SPAIN
AND
PORTUGAL

Cultures and Costumes Series:

SPAIN
AND
PORTUGAL

KEITH STUART

MASON CREST PUBLISHERS

www.masoncrest.com

Mason Crest Publishers Inc.
370 Reed Road
Broomall, PA 19008
(866) MCP-BOOK (toll free)
www.masoncrest.com

First printing 2002

1 2 3 4 5 6 7 8 9 10

Library of Congress Cataloging-in-Publication Data available

ISBN 1-59084-440-8

Printed and bound in Malaysia

Editorial and design by
Amber Books Ltd.
Bradley's Close
74–77 White Lion Street
London N1 9PF

Project Editor: Marie-Claire Muir
Designer: Hawes Design
Picture Research: Lisa Wren

Picture Credits:
All pictures courtesy of Amber Books Ltd, except the following:
Mary Evans Picture Library: 48.

ACKNOWLEDGMENT
For authenticating this book, the Publishers would like to thank
Robert L. Humphrey, Jr., Professor Emeritus of Anthropology,
George Washington University, Washington, D.C.

Contents

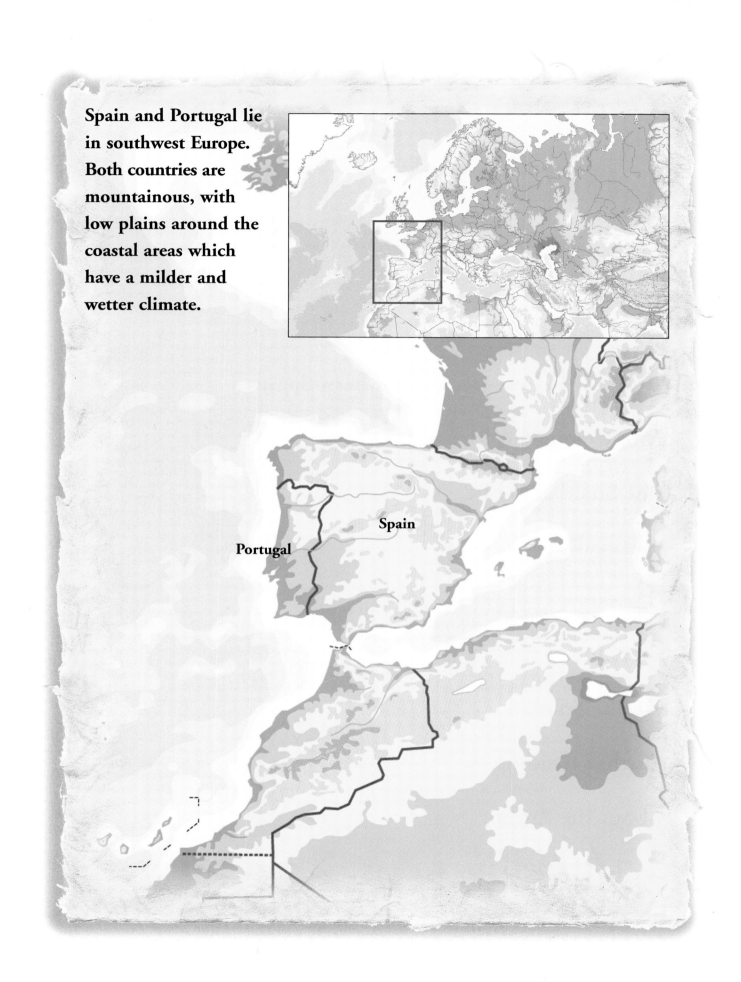

Spain and Portugal lie in southwest Europe. Both countries are mountainous, with low plains around the coastal areas which have a milder and wetter climate.

Spain

Portugal

Introduction

Nearly every species in the animal kingdom adapts to changes in the environment. To cope with cold weather, the cat adapts by growing a longer coat of fur, the bear hibernates, and birds migrate to a different climatic zone. Only humans use costume and culture—what they have learned through many generations—to adapt to the environment.

The first humans developed their culture by using spears to hunt the bear, knives and scrapers to skin it, and needles and sinew to turn the hide into a warm coat to insulate their hairless bodies. As time went on, the clothes humans wore became an indicator of cultural and individual differences. Some were clearly developed to be more comfortable in the environment, others were designed for decorative, economic, political, and religious reasons.

Ritual costumes can tell us about the deities, ancestors, and civil and military ranking in a society, while other clothing styles can identify local or national identity. Social class, gender, age, economic status, climate, profession, and political persuasion are also reflected in clothing. Anthropologists have even tied changes in the hemline length of women's dresses to periods of cultural stress or relative calm.

In 13 beautifully illustrated volumes, the *Cultures and Costumes: Symbols of their Period* series explores the remarkable variety of costumes found around the world and through different eras. Each book shows how different societies have clothed themselves, revealing a wealth of diverse and sometimes mystifying explanations. Costume can be used as a social indicator by scientists, artists, cinematographers, historians, and designers—and also provide students with a better understanding of their own and other cultures.

ROBERT L. HUMPHREY, JR., Professor Emeritus of Anthropology,
George Washington University, Washington, D.C.

Spain: A Past of Many Parts

Since around 700 B.C., the area now known as Spain has been invaded and occupied by a long succession of peoples as different as Celts and Moors. Each has left its own lasting impression on this land of contrasts.

The country of Spain takes up most of the Iberian Peninsula, a rectangular stretch of land that juts out southwest from continental Europe into the Atlantic Ocean. Hundreds of years before Christ, the Celts rampaged through the Pyrenees Mountains and settled in the north. Then the ancient Greeks began setting up trading posts on the southern coast as they sailed along the Strait of Gibraltar, a narrow strip of sea between Spain and Africa.

Between 206 B.C. and A.D. 400, Spain became part of the Roman Empire. However, when that began to crumble, the country was invaded, first by barbarians, and then by the Visigoths, a tribe of Germanic origin. In A.D. 711, an army of invading Moors from North Africa defeated the Visigoth king, Roderick, and quickly captured most of the peninsula.

These figures are from 13th-century Spain. Their lengthy robes are richly colored and reveal the wearers to be wealthy noblemen and women. Peasants would have worn more practical, short tunics.

Rich women of medieval Spain wore long, simply designed robes and tall head-dresses. They were well known for their long, curly hair. The men's robes are shorter, and their pointed shoes show a Moorish influence.

Soon, Christianity was spreading through Spain, and Christian kings began to take control of the country region by region. The first major Catholic provinces were Castile, León, and Aragón. However, gaining control of the whole country was a long process, and the Moors held onto their final stronghold of Granada in the southeast of the country until 1492. Modern Spain still bears the signs of its varied past, with each successive invader leaving its own marks on the culture, architecture, and costume of the country.

The Clothes of Early Spain

During the Middle Ages, Spain was caught between two distinct worlds. From the north, European travelers brought French and Italian fashions into the country as they made pilgrimages to Santiago de Compostela, where the remains of Saint James the Apostle are buried. At the same time, the Moors still

controlled the south of Spain. From the region known at the time as Al Andalus—now Andalucía—came beautiful textiles and fashions, quite different from those found in the rest of Europe.

Most importantly, the Moors brought silk to Spain, which was extremely difficult to come by elsewhere in Europe. At first, it was imported from North Africa, but later, it was actually produced in Al Andalus. Here, the Moors built silk mills and grew mulberry trees, the leaves of which are eaten by silkworms. This luxurious fabric became popular with Christian noblemen and -women alike, and also with the clergy. Merchants would take either raw silk, or silk fashioned into garments, and transport it to the north by river.

The basic clothing throughout Europe at this time was the cloth tunic, a sleeveless and shapeless garment, usually tied around the waist. Twelfth-century Spain produced its own version, called the *brial,* which was typically cut to knee length for men and longer for women. A North African influence was obvious in the use of fine silks.

Over the *brial* was worn a version of the Roman *pallium*. This was a type of short, squarish cloak fastened around the upper chest with a gold chain. In the 13th century, a long, sleeveless robe called a surcoat, or *pellotes,* became fashionable. Rich Spanish ladies decorated their robes with lace and Arabian brocade—a fine, silky fabric often woven with silver or gold thread. Other textiles used during this age included leather and animal pelts. Rabbit skin was popular as a comfortable lining inside clothes.

The Golden Age

Christopher Columbus (1451–1506), the Italian-born navigator and explorer, arrived at one of the islands off Cuba on October 12, 1492, thus rediscovering the Americas for his patrons, Ferdinand and Isabella of Spain. For the next 50 years, Spanish sailors ventured to and from the New World, conquering the areas now known as Mexico, Cuba, Venezuela, Paraguay, Colombia, Bolivia, and Chile, and then sailing on farther north to Florida.

Colonists soon discovered that South America was rich with deposits of silver and gold. The precious metals were mined and shipped back to Spain in considerable quantities, thereby swelling the royal coffers. Then, in 1580, Portugal and all its lucrative colonies in India and Africa

Europe's Best Wool

From the Middle Ages until the 18th century, wool was a vital element of the Spanish economy. Spain's merino sheep produced the best wool in Europe—soft, comfortable, and strong. Sheep could be reared on land unsuitable for agriculture, so wool production supported thousands of peasant families. Unsurprisingly, farmers were banned from exporting their sheep to other countries.

fell under Spanish sovereignty following the death of King Sebastian of Portugal during a foolhardy crusade against the Moors in Morocco. For a brief period, Spain became the greatest empire in the world and, consequently, the most fashionable.

Suddenly, all of civilized Europe was looking to Spain for new trends in dress. For gentlewomen came the farthingale (*verdugado* in Spanish). This was an underskirt designed to swell out from the waist by means of a series of hoops that were originally made from unseasoned wood—hence the name, which is derived from *verdugo*, Spanish for "green stick." The hoops grew in circumference toward the feet to form a bell shape. A layer of petticoats and an overdress covered this cumbersome garment.

There is some contention among historians about exactly when the farthingale made its way from Spain to other parts of Europe. Some believe Catherine of Aragón introduced the style to England in 1501. Others argue it was in 1554, when Mary

This intricately etched suit of armor is very much in the Gothic style, with depictions of gargoyles covering the surface. The heavy design work would have limited the armor's protective capabilities.

This suit is inspired by the Maximilian style of fluted armor that came from Germany in the early 16th century. The style is named after the Holy Roman Emperor Maximilian (1459–1519).

Tudor, daughter of Catherine and King Henry VIII, married Philip II of Spain. Whatever the truth, the style was popular and remained fashionable for many years, although the French and Italians regularly refined it, including the introduction of whalebone hoops.

New Styles for Men

Proud of their country's great empire, Spanish noblemen wanted clothes that emphasized their stature and bearing. Consequently, a high, stiff collar came into fashion that forced the wearer to literally keep his head held high. With the high collar came the ruff, an elaborate, round, frilly neck decoration that was fashionable for both men and women.

At first, the ruff was small, perhaps two inches (5 cm) wide. As the 16th century went on, it grew to be more and more pronounced. *Portrait of a Lady*, painted by Spanish artist Pantoja de la Cruz around 1640, shows a woman wearing a ruff that is at least 25 inches (63 cm) in diameter. This was entirely impractical, but that was the point. The wearer wanted to tell the world that he or she did not have to do any work for themselves. Impractical meant rich.

To emphasize a masculine look, men also wore padded **doublets** (this was known as the peascod-belly style) and short, puffed-out **breeches** with prominent **codpieces**.

Staunchly Catholic

When the Catholic monarchs Ferdinand of Aragón and Isabella of Castile defeated the Moors at Granada in 1492, it marked the end of 500 years of religious warfare. Because of this struggle, Spain became a particularly zealous guardian of the Catholic faith. During the infamous Spanish Inquisition, which began in 1480 and went on until 1808, suspected **heretics**, Jews, Muslims, and Protestants were interrogated, exiled, or often executed under the direction of a small group of officers, or inquisitors, controlled by the Crown. The country also took part in the Crusades against the Muslim Ottoman Empire in the mid-1500s. Spain's strong religious piety had an important effect on the costume of its people.

Apart from the brief period of ostentation during the boom years of the empire, the aristocracy of the country acquired a reputation for somber, almost **ecclesiastical**, dress, employing dark colors and simple designs. In his influential book, *The Courier* (1528), Count Baldassare Castiglione suggested that all European noblemen should adopt the somber Spanish look and refrain from dressing in frivolous colors more commonly associated with court jesters. However, although some historians suggest that this dark attire did become fashionable throughout Europe during the 16th century, it is debatable how much of an influence it had on the more flamboyant courts, such as those of Italy and France.

By the early 17th century, Spain was seeing its riches disappear because of a series of expensive wars, so it became necessary to make cutbacks. In 1623, King Philip IV decided to made black, simple clothing the official uniform of the royal court to reflect the solemn times. In a portrait by Diego Velázquez, the king is dressed entirely in black and, instead of a large, showy ruff around his neck, he is wearing a plain stiff collar. Spain's days of leading the fashions of Europe had ended.

The Nobleman in Armor

During the 16th century, at the height of the Spanish empire, military pride was an important element of noble society. Until the English fleet destroyed the Spanish Armada in 1588, Spain had not been defeated in a battle for 150 years. The country was enjoying successes in South America and against the Muslim Turks, who were looking to extend their Ottoman Empire into Christian Europe.

Consequently, a nobleman's armor was a potent symbol of his wealth and power, like a high-powered sports car today. Often, suits were specially made to wear in parades instead of in battle. These suits were lavishly decorated with intricate etchings. Charles V and Philip II of Spain had suits of armor decorated for them by the finest etchers in Europe, including Ulrich Holzmann and Hans Burgkmair the Younger.

It was in the 16th century that armor reached its technical peak. Suits were made with many **articulated** plates around the joints so that the wearer could move freely but still be protected at the knees, elbows, and shoulders. Horse armor, or "bardings," were also highly advanced. A shaped metal plate called a *chanfron* protected the horse's face and eyes, a series of articulated plates covered its neck, and a *peytral* made of steel or thick leather covered its body. The best armor was made in Germany and Italy, so Spain imported a lot of its armor from these countries, although there were armor workshops in several Spanish cities, including Barcelona and Seville.

The key weapon of the mounted soldier was the one-handed sword, or rapier. This weapon had a long, double-edged blade designed to penetrate an enemy's armor. To protect the hand, the handle, or "grip," of the weapon was frequently surrounded by a system of **guard arms**, often in an S shape. Again, noblemen liked to show off their wealth with a finely etched or engraved sword. As a result, the guard arms became more and more elaborate.

Spanish kings and noblemen of the 16th century protected their horses, as well as themselves, with articulated steel armor. They would also carry a short sword with an S-shaped hand guard (inset) and a long spear or pike.

The clothing of these 18th-century revelers, playing Blind Man's Bluff, is colorful. The men's velvet breeches and coats are deep reds, blues, and yellows. The ladies' skirts are white muslin with distinctive horizontal stripes.

Goya and Spanish Fashion

In 1774, King Charles III commissioned the brilliant Spanish painter Francisco Goya to work on a selection of **cartoons** that were later to be copied into tapestries at the Royal Tapestry Factory of Santa Bárbara. He chose Madrid's lively fiesta of San Isidro as one of his subjects and went about portraying the costumes and antics of both rich and poor as they enjoyed the festivities.

Goya's painting *Blind Man's Bluff* (1788) shows a group of young people playing the popular party game. Their costumes take French and English fashions and mix them with local styles, which was typical of Spain at this time. The women are wearing two types of hat common throughout Europe. The girl at the back has a wide-brimmed hat with a stiff crown and a large ostrich feather adorning the side—a popular style from the mid-century onward. The other ladies are wearing variations on the softer mobcap, which was seen throughout the 18th century. These were often full and frilly, made from linen, lace, or muslin and decorated with ribbons.

Their skirts are clearly no longer bulked out by the hooped farthingale, which was falling out of favor at this time. From the 1770s on, many women in France and Italy switched to the bustle—a form of whalebone belt with a large protrusion at the back. This was worn under the skirts to give a fuller profile without the discomfort of the farthingale or the later French **pannier,** However, the skirts in Goya's painting have no bustle either. In fact, these garments show a complete departure from French tastes. They are light, almost see-through, and are short enough to reveal the feet, which was rare in European fashion during this era.

This form of dress was inspired by the *maja,* a name given to the brazen, lower-class young women of Madrid who flouted the gentile dress of the era. (Goya's most famous painting is *The Naked Maja.*) They wore their hair unpowdered and favored shorter skirts without hoops to alter their silhouette. Many have suggested that the look began with Spain's Gypsy communities.

The men are all wearing variations on what was standard male dress for most of the 18th century: coat, vest, and breeches worn over stockings. However, their coats look more like the short *chaquetilla* the matadors wore.

Improvements in Makeup

By the end of the 18th century, the thick, white paste that women once used as makeup (often to cover blemishes caused by smallpox) was going out of fashion—not least because the amount of lead and mercury it often contained was doing the skin more harm than good. Instead, scientific advances in cosmetics were producing much safer, kinder alternatives. One popular product was "Spanish wool." Oil extracted from the wool of Spain's merino sheep was used to create rouge, which added a reddish color to the cheeks and lips.

Traditional Costumes of Southern Spain

The invading tribes that have passed through each region of Spain have greatly affected them. In the south, it was the Moors who made the greatest impression, bringing African and Arabic food, science, and architecture, as well as clothing. Their rich textiles, exotic fashions, and unique decorative techniques influenced Spanish fashions from the eighth century onward.

Modern Spain is divided into 17 regions. For much of the country's complicated history, these were separate kingdoms with different rulers and dialects. Alfonso VI, in the 11th and 12th centuries, was the first king to declare himself emperor of all Spain. However, when he died, the land was split

The traditional clothes of Minorca and Majorca are similar. The women wear full cotton skirts with stripes or floral designs and *robozilla* headdresses. The men wear baggy breeches tucked in at the knees. Designs are usually simple but colorful.

between his sons, and infighting saw the country continually divided and subdivided. In the 17th century, Philip IV of Castile sought to build a unified Spain under his power. Even now, however, the regions retain their distinctly independent character. Catalonia, the Basque country, and Galicia even have their own languages.

Traditional costumes worn by working people into the early 20th century are perhaps where various ethnic influences are most obvious, although now these garments are usually only seen during fiestas.

Murcia

Situated on the southeastern coast of Spain, Murcia is primarily an agricultural region, its warm climate perfect for growing fruits, such as lemons, peaches, and apricots. The Murcian people once had a reputation for being hardworking

Spain's Gypsy Community

The Romany Gypsies—or *gitano* as they are known in Spanish—are a **nomadic** people originally from northern India. They began settling in Spain, especially Murcia and Andalucía, in the Middle Ages and carved out livings for themselves as blacksmiths, musicians, horse traders, and fortune tellers. Of course, the Gypsies brought their own varied costumes, too. Most famously, women wore frilled sleeves and tiered skirts in vibrant colors—a direct influence on the Sevillana dress now associated with flamenco. The men wore velvet hats and jackets, frilled white shirts, and wide sashes. After 1492, the Gypsies—like the Moors and Jews—became subject to persecution and were often forced to live apart from Christians. In 1783, an edict (law) was passed banning traditional Gypsy clothing. Today, however, these settlers are recognized as an important influence on Spanish culture.

yet somewhat morose. Now tourists enjoy the laid-back atmosphere, and the region is enlivened by a busy calendar of fiestas. It is also an excellent place to learn about the costumes of Spain. Every year between September 6 and 9, Murcia holds an International Festival of Mediterranean Folklore. Hundreds of people wear traditional clothing from throughout southern Spain, making for one of the most colorful events in the country.

In contrast, the traditional dress of the region is simple and modest. Men wear the obligatory sombrero over a padded kerchief that resembles a small turban. Around the waist is a broad red *faja,* or sash—again, a typical feature of Spanish clothing. Knee-length breeches are worn with striped blue stockings and *alpargatas,* or **espadrilles**, tied with ribbons. The Murcian farmer would also have carried a jacket decorated with embroidery and *passementaries*—trimmings of gold or silver lace. This is similar to garments worn in nearby Andalucía, and the lavish decoration suggests a Moorish influence.

As for women, the hairstyle is of most interest. Two braids are rolled into buns on either side of the head, and a small comb secures the arrangement. A flower, perhaps a red carnation or a dahlia, is used for decoration. Carnations are a popular decorative flower throughout Spain and are often used as hair ornaments by flamenco dancers.

During the Feria de Primavera, or Spring Festival, there is a carnival through the streets

This couple are from the countryside near the border with Castille La Mancha. The woman's skirt is comparatively short, revealing white stockings. The colors are muted, with only the yellow of her top and the man's red *faja* standing out.

of the city of Murcia, where young women wear the area's traditional fiesta dress—a full skirt with heavy floral embroidery along the hem, a white corsage, and an elaborate white lace apron with matching *fichu*. A red carnation at the top of the dress, beneath the neck, is a must.

Valencia

The region of Valencia, like its neighbor Murcia, is renowned for its agricultural produce, especially oranges, which the Moors brought to Spain. Along the coast are acres of rich **alluvial plains**, where farmers have been cultivating rice since the Middle Ages. This is where Spain's national dish, *paella*, was invented.

The most distinctive traditional apparel of Valencia is a long, garishly colored woolen blanket that the men wear over their shoulders. This striped garment has dozens of uses: food can be rolled up in it, money can be hidden in it, and it can provide a warm cape if the temperature drops. The blanket is usually worn with the familiar vest and breeches, and a pair of espadrilles, which are made from beaten hemp.

Modest materials, such as wool, linen, and cotton, dominate the traditional clothing of Valencian working men. However, their waistcoats are brocaded, and the *fajas* are sometimes made of silk.

Valencian farmers once also wore a white linen garment that reached down to the knees. It is thought that this attire had ancient Greek origins, because Greek sailors established trading posts down the coast of Valencia in around 700 B.C. This garment is certainly unlike anything else in the region. A tall straw hat with a narrow rim, along with a white shirt and short vest, may also have accompanied the linen skirt.

Traditionally, the women of Valencia wear pastel-colored dresses, embellished with aprons and *fichus* of fine lace or brocade, and flounced lace cuffs. Pink and blue bows are also popular, both as fasteners for the apron and *fichu,* and as decorative additions to the sleeves of the dress. White shoes with low heels and white stockings are typical too. Plenty of gold jewelry—earrings, necklaces, and pendants—is also a mandatory part of the Valencian fiesta.

The Balearic Islands

This beautiful **archipelago** off the east coast of Spain has been colonized by the Greeks, Romans, Goths, Vandals, and Moors, but came under the rule of Aragón in the 14th century. Since then, the British occupied Minorca for a brief period, but the island group is now a province of Spain. The main islands are Majorca, Minorca, Ibiza, Formentera, and Cabrera. Historically, the people of the Balearics were farmers and craftsmen, exporting wool, pottery, and woven baskets to the mainland. Most income now comes from tourism.

Although these islands have a surface area of barely 1,900 square miles (5,000 sq km), the history of costume here is rich and diverse. Styles have been taken from many invaders and adapted over the years. The relative isolation of the Balearics has allowed some peculiar fashions to evolve, many of which, unfortunately, have been lost. The prolific and controversial French author George Sand visited the islands in 1837, and in her book, *A Winter in Mallorca,* she commented on how upper-class women had abandoned traditional clothing altogether in favor of cosmopolitan European styles. Some remnants lived on, however, in the clothing of the peasants.

We know that these women are either peasants or servants, as these were the only groups who wore aprons. The woman on the right wears a variation of the *robozilla* on her head.

The most interesting item of local attire is the women's headwear. The *robozilla* is a kind of cowl (hood) that covers the head and shoulders and attaches under the chin so that only the face can be seen. The *robozilla* is usually made from **batiste** and embroidered with floral patterns. It can also be decorated around the neck with a ruff or fanned **gorget** of silk—these suggest the headdress has its origins in the 16th century, when ruffs became fashionable throughout Europe. Some of the traditional men's clothing of the islands has been influenced by the same period. Until the end of the 19th century, farmers still wore the short, puffed-out breeches that were popular in mainland Spain in the mid-1500s.

Hints of Africa and Arabia

There are also North African influences in Balearic attire. In 18th-century

The traditional clothes of Majorca resemble those of the mainland. The woman on the left has an arabesque design along the hem of her skirt. The woman on the right wears a version of the classic Spanish *mantilla*.

Minorca, men were spotted wearing a long tunic, ankle-length cotton trousers, and a large red coat over the shoulders. The tunic is similar to the caftan, a long cotton garment favored throughout North Africa and the Middle East, and certain to have been worn by Moorish invaders. Furthermore, the robe resembles the *bisht,* or *mishlah,* an Arabian cloak that is worn draped over the shoulders.

Unmarried girls from Ibiza once wore an abundance of necklaces decorated with coins, and these typically represented the **dowry** that would be offered to the bridegroom. This, too, could have been adopted from Moorish settlers. The Berber women of North Africa wear headdresses and necklaces lined with silver coins, and in some areas of Morocco, this handmade jewelry represents the wealth of the girl's family. The women of Portugal's Minho region, which was likewise colonized by North African invaders, once also adopted this custom.

By the beginning of the 20th century, Balearic attire had come more into line with the rest of Spain. The men's baggy trousers, sometimes striped and usually colored in earthy browns and greens, were accompanied by tight vests, white shirts, and a handkerchief knotted around the neck. Women wore a black silk **corset** with tight sleeves, stockings, and a full skirt. They also retained the distinctive *robozilla*. This must have been uncomfortably warm at times, considering the Mediterranean climate. Unsurprisingly, the fan was an essential accessory.

Spain's National Garment

The *mantilla*—a lace shawl designed to cover the shoulders and sometimes the head as well—has become inextricably associated with Spain, especially the southern region of Andalucía. Some argue that the garment has its origins in headdresses worn by the Iberians, a tribe that populated the peninsula during the Bronze Age a few thousand years before Christ. It may also have been inspired by the various veils and headdresses Moorish women brought to Spain during the early Middle Ages. These are still a feature of Muslim dress today.

However, the *mantilla* did not achieve mass popularity until the 16th century, when it was adopted and adapted by different regions and classes. At first, cloth and sometimes even velvet were used, but lace became the preferred fabric in the 18th century. Many of the portraits painted by Spanish artist Francisco Goya show women in fine lace *mantillas*—they were particularly popular among Madrid's fashionable young *maja* women. In that era, the garment was often worn as a type of headscarf, pinned to the hair with a tortoiseshell comb, or *peineta*.

During the 1800s, the *mantilla* reached the height of its popularity. It even achieved political significance in the 1870s, when noblewomen protesting against the policies of King Amadeo de Saboya wore it as a symbol of defiance.

When hats became more fashionable in the latter years of the century, the *mantilla* fell out of favor in much of Spain. It remained popular in Andalucía and Castile, however, especially during special occasions. The black *mantilla* was associated with solemn religious events and holy days, while the white *mantilla* was usually worn during fiestas and especially bullfights.

Two types of lace are used to make *mantillas*. Chantilly is a delicate, filmy material first produced in the French town of the same name. It tends to be used to make the black *mantillas* worn on religious days. Blond lace is stronger and heavier and is used for white *mantillas*.

These Minorcan and Majorcan costumes show the use of contrasting colors and patterns among the islands' inhabitants. Stripes and floral designs were popular.

Folk Costumes of the North

Far away from Andalucía, the political and cultural capital of Moorish Spain, other tribes left their marks. Their legacy is reflected in the traditional dress of the central and northern regions alongside the inescapable imprint of the Moors.

Spain saw the arrival of the Celts from across the Pyrenees in around 700 B.C. They brought with them elements of their singular culture, most noticeable in the folk dances and musical instruments of Galicia. In 801 A.D., the Franks—a Germanic tribe that had conquered Gaul (modern-day France) in the sixth century A.D.—invaded Catalonia and occupied Barcelona, bringing a new language and new influences.

Catalonia

Set in the far northeastern corner of Spain, bordering France and the Mediterranean Sea, Catalonia is almost a country in its own right. The language contains as many elements of French as it does Castilian Spanish, and

Traditionally, Catalan dress tempers the usually colorful Spanish styles with black accessories: for women, black mittens, black hairnets, and often black aprons; for men, black breeches and jackets.

the region has its own police force and a powerful local government. The people see themselves as Catalán first, Spanish second.

Most areas of Catalonia have their own traditional costumes, which were worn as everyday dress into the early 20th century. In line with the proud, independent attitude of the people, there are some individual features. The men, for example, wear a distinctive woolen stocking cap, typically in red or black. This is a modification of the **Phrygian bonnet** that came out of Asia Minor between 1000 and 500 B.C. and was adopted by the ancient Persians, Greeks, and Romans. Originally, the hat was pointed and conical, but the Catalán version is folded, usually toward the front. Variations on this bonnet can be found throughout the Mediterranean.

Catalán men can also be seen carrying a short jacket over one shoulder. This is not just a casual gesture; it is a tribute to the Miquelets, a famously tough and committed Catalán army regiment that fought against the French in various territorial disputes between the 17th and 19th centuries. Part of the uniform was a short **frock coat** that was always worn on their shoulders—the men never put their arms through the sleeves.

The rest of the costume tends to look stylish and ostentatious: a short jacket, breeches buttoned at the sides, a wide sash, buttoned vest, and embroidered tie. Sometimes, bright blue velvet is used for the breeches and jacket; other times, the outfit is almost entirely black and made from local merino wool.

A peasant from Castile: his military-style rough cloth coat and hat hint at the region's war-torn past. Castile—meaning "castle"—has seen many battles between Christians and Moors.

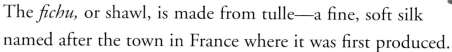

Two women from the region of Asturias. The lady on the right is from a more mountainous area, so her clothes are made from thick wool. For milder areas, textiles are lighter and styles more decorative.

Apart from the essential black blouse, the women's clothing is similarly colorful and flamboyant. Skirts and aprons are stylishly patterned in plaids or lush floral designs. The *fichu,* or shawl, is made from tulle—a fine, soft silk named after the town in France where it was first produced. It is richly embroidered and stitched with gold sequins. Gold and silver jewelry is plentiful, too, and large and ornate dangling earrings are the most important of these. The style is most likely Berber in origin. Finally, instead of the *mantilla*-style headdress, women sometimes wear a long black hairnet. This style was especially popular during the 18th century—two of the girls in Goya's *Blind Man's Bluff* sketch are wearing them.

Elements of traditional dress are still worn today for special occasions, especially during performances of the *sardana,* Catalonia's national dance. This exact, graceful dance is performed in a ring with participants holding hands. Even when modern clothing is worn, the traditional **alpargatas** with ribbons that lace up the ankle remain popular.

Asturias

It was in this geographically varied region that the Christian resistance against the Moors began. Troops under the command of the Visigoth King Pelayo defeated Muslim soldiers at Covadonga in A.D. 722, marking the first victory of the **_Reconquista_**. As with Galicia, there is a strong Celtic influence in the music and dance of the region.

Traditional Asturian dress is still worn during the International Fair in the town of Fuengirola, as well as at various other fiestas and musical events. Male costume is usually a white, open-necked shirt, black vest, and a black cap. A white vest with brown shoulders is one alternative. You might also see Celtic musicians wearing a conical hat similar to the one that Galician

dancers wore, but without the pom-poms. This is related to the cone-shaped hats the ancient Celts wore.

Women wear a white blouse and red skirt with black borders—again, similar to the designs from other northern regions, such as Galicia and the Basque country. The women also cover their heads with a head scarf, either plain or with floral designs.

The Basque Country

Isolated by its mountainous location, the Basque country has a different history from the rest of Spain. The Basques are thought to be the last remnants of a tribe that lived in Europe between 10,000 and 75,000 years ago. Although the

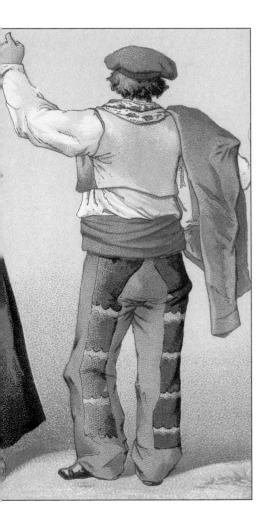

exact origins of this people are a mystery, the Basque language—Euskera—is unique, predating the Roman occupation of the Iberian Peninsula. Divided into seven provinces, the most northern of which spills over into France, the Basque country is defiantly independent-minded.

The traditional peasant woman's dress is similar to that of Galicia. The voluminous red skirt has black bands around the hem and is covered by a plain black apron. An equally plain bodice is laced up the front and worn over a high-necked white blouse with long sleeves. There are variations,

The family in the center of this group is from Aragón, the others are Basques. The women's clothes are similar, with red, brown, and black borders. The men's hats show different influences: the Basque beret from France and the broad-brimmed hat from southern Spain.

however, such as a bright-colored blouse with a pattern around the short sleeves. Basque women would also usually have cotton kerchiefs that cover most of their hair.

The most interesting elements of the traditional male costume are the large red beret, worn angled to one side, and long trousers decorated on the front and back with colored velvet patches, although a plain pair of baggy white trousers is more usual. A broad red sash, white vest, and billowing white shirt with a large collar are the usual accompaniments. The Basque country has literally hundreds of folk dances, most with their own slightly different costumes; however, the use of a white shirt and trousers with red sash and beret is almost universal. This outfit is similar to that worn by English morris dancers. Many Basque folk dances, like the **morris dances**, have their roots in pagan rituals of fertility.

The wealthy country women of Castile's Salamanca province were once famous for their elaborately decorated costumes, complete with gold embroidery and numerous gold necklaces, chains, and pendants. They earned the nickname *charro,* which meant gaudy or ostentatious.

Castile

Castile, by far the country's largest region, is split into two provinces: Castile-León and Castile-La Mancha. This was once the power center of Christian Spain, the homeland of great kings. The region boasts an astonishingly varied landscape, from arid deserts to craggy mountains. It also contains some of Spain's most beautiful cities, including Toledo, Burgos, and Salamanca.

Traditional dress varies widely from province to province, but there are some recurring themes. For women, skirts, and sometimes blouses, are

Arabesque

Arabesque refers to an Arabian technique of decoration that consists of intricate geometric patterns that repeat and interlock across the surface of an object or garment. Islamic law forbids the representation of humans or animals in art, and this highly elaborate style evolved as a result. Complex shapes and floral motifs are common themes.

Muslim Moors brought arabesque into Spain, and it made a lasting impression on the fashions of the country. Examples of the technique are found in the country's Moorish architecture, as well as its traditional clothing.

A Maragato wears the peoples' traditional dress. Two statues wearing this outfit can be seen sounding the chimes on the famous Town Hall clock in Astorga.

decorated with appliqué—decorative cloth stitched onto the surface of another fabric. In Castile, gold-lined black velvet, cut into designs, such as flowers, leaves, and branches, is added to the base of skirts.

Sometimes, the recurring designs are embroidered directly onto the skirt using black thread. This technique, known as blackwork, was immensely fashionable throughout Europe in the 16th century. The style, brought to England by Catherine of Aragón, was often referred to as "Spanish work," because it was thought to have originated in Spain. However, the often-arabesque designs suggest that the technique may have originated with the Moors.

The *mantón de Manila* has also been associated with the traditional dress of Castile. This is a large silk shawl colorfully embroidered with floral patterns and completed with fringes or tassels along the edges. The garment was first brought to Spain from Manila when the Philippines became part of the Spanish empire during the reign of Philip II. It quickly became an essential, if somewhat expensive, item.

Perhaps the most interesting people of Castile are the Maragatos, a rugged, independent tribe believed to be of mixed Barber–Visigoth descent. During the Middle Ages, the Maragatos settled near Mount Teleno in the region of León and never intermarried with Spaniards outside their **caste**. Their descendants still live in the area, which is now known as La Maragatería. The standard dress of the Maragatos is baggy breeches, **gaiters**, a long, dark jacket tightened at the waist with a broad belt, and a broad rimmed hat.

Aragón

Bordered by mountains to the north and south, Aragón is a harsh, although beautiful, region. It was populated by a famously tough-minded people—descendants, perhaps, of the combative Celtiberian tribes that inhabited the area thousands of years ago. Liberated from the Moors in the 13th century, Aragón went on to play a key role in the rise of Christian Spain when Ferdinand of Aragón married Queen Isabella of Castile in 1469. A Moorish flavor remains, however, in the **mudéjar** architecture of Turuel and Zaragoza and in some elements of the clothing.

Aragón is probably best known for its local folk dance, the energetic, fast-paced *jota*. Performed in couples, it is a regular sight at the region's fiestas, especially the Virgen del Pilar fiesta in October. The traditional costume for the dance dates back to the 18th century. For women, this consists of a pleated woolen skirt with a velvet band around the hem, a small apron of black silk, and a black velvet bodice with long sleeves. A colorful cotton *fichu* is worn, too, but it is relatively plain compared to the extravagant sequined versions of neighboring Catalonia. The male dress is more varied, but usually includes an unbuttoned white shirt, a velvet or corduroy vest with no buttons, and *alpargatas* fastened with black ribbons. The trousers are just over knee-length and often worn over a pair of white cotton long johns or *pololos*.

Madrid: The Stylish City

Madrid is Spain's capital city. Every year during the festival of San Isidro, dozens of people put on the traditional dress of Madrid, the *chulapo* for men and the *chulapa* for women. Many enter an annual competition to decide who is the most stylish. The men wear a flat, white and blue checkered cap with matching vest and cravat. Women wear a long dress with lace frills and an extravagantly embroidered *manton de Manila*.

The Spanish Fiesta

Spain is a lively and vibrant country where exuberant street celebrations, known as fiestas, provide regular high points throughout the year. There are numerous events that are celebrated nationwide, but also countless local fiestas specific to individual towns and villages, where dressing up in traditional regional costume is an important part of the celebration

Most fiestas are celebrations of national religious festivals, like All Saints' Day on November 1 and Holy Week, or *Semana Santa*—the week preceding Easter. However, there are also many local fiestas that might only be celebrated in a single town. These often have their foundations in medieval ritual and drama. The Mystery of Elche, for example, is a medieval mystery play performed in the city of Elche's cathedral every August. Several towns also stage events in which participants in historical dress reenact important local battles between the Moors and the Christians.

Each highly elaborate bullfighting costume is entirely handmade by a small team of tailors and can cost the equivalent of 3,000 dollars. It will take a matador over an hour to get dressed before the *corrida*.

Favorite colors for the *traje de luces* include blue, yellow, red, and pink—bright hues that contrast with the *corrida* sand, the heaving crowds, and the dark bulls. The garments are tight fitting so they do not hinder movement.

Bullfighting

Bullfighting remains an essential part of Spanish culture. Whenever a town or city holds a fiesta, the bullfight—or *corrida* as it is usually known—will usually be a central part of the celebration. Bullfighting is a cross between theater, ballet, and ritual—some say it symbolizes the triumph of man's wit and intelligence over the brute force of nature. The bullfight can be traced back to the Middle Ages, when it was originally a pastime for noblemen on horseback, like fox hunting in England. When the practice fell out of favor with the aristocracy, servants and working-class people, who fought the bulls on foot, took it up. Over the centuries, the bullfight became more and more ritualized, and the bullfighters themselves—known as matadors—turned into folk heroes.

The Costume of the *Corrida*

Matadors take great pride in their costumes, which are an important aspect of the event. The traditional costume is the *traje de luces,* or "suit of light," which refers to the way in which sunlight sparkles off the gold and silver adornments that cover the material. The style of the suit goes back to the 18th century, but has gone through many refinements since. It is usually made from brightly colored silks and satins, and consists of several mandatory elements. The most important is the *chaquetilla,* a short jacket covered in decorative gold and silver clasps and rich embroidery. The *chaquetilla,* sometimes also known as a *bolero,* has extravagant shoulder pads and slits beneath the armpits to aid the movement of the matador, because the fabric is quite rigid.

Next are the *taleguilla,* the matador's satin breeches. These are often made with a light-colored fabric—usually in pink, yellow, green, or blue—and are embroidered with rich patterns on the sides. The *taleguilla* can be adjusted with tassels called *machos.* A pair of silk stockings is also worn, often of the same pastel colors as the breeches.

Beneath the *chaquetilla* is the *camisa,* the matador's shirt, which is white and also embroidered. Around the collar of the *camisa* is the *corbatín,* a thin necktie that can be plain or patterned. Black slippers, *zapatillas,* complete the outfit. These have special soles to ensure the matador does not slip or slide. The last part of the outfit is the *montera,* the matador's cap. Before the last century, a stiff three-cornered hat was favored, but now the cap is made from softer black velvet, perhaps decorated with pom-poms. The matador will often toss the *montera* into the crowd after a successful fight.

In addition to the *traje de luces,* the matador has several important accessories. In the procession that comes before a bullfight, the matador wears the luxurious *capote de paseo,* a large, extravagant cape that is heavily illustrated, often with religious figures. This is then replaced by a standard cape—the *capote*—which is used to goad the bull during the beginning of the third stage of the fight. When the matador is ready to perform the kill, he exchanges the capote for a smaller, more practical, red cape, referred to as the *muleta,* and the *estoque*—the short, curved sword with which the matador makes his final blow.

Other *Corrida* Characters

The nature of the bullfight varies from region to region, but classically, the event is split into three 15-minute stages. In the first stage, men on horseback, called *picadors,* jab at the bull with long spears, weakening it. These riders dress similarly to the matadors, with elaborately embroidered jackets, vests, and breeches. There are some key differences, however. Instead of a *montera,* the *picador* wears a broad-brimmed felt hat decorated with a ball of ribbons. Sturdy leather trousers replace the matador's satin breeches, and *picadors* also wear steel guards on their feet to protect against the bull's horns.

In the second stage of the fight, a group of assistant bullfighters, known as *banderilleros,* stab brightly colored, barbed sticks called *banderilleras* into the bull's back, which stick in the skin and aggravate the animal. To signify the lower rank of the banderilleros, their jackets and trousers are decorated with only black braids and embroidery, lacking the gold and silver adornments of the matador's outfit. Finally, the matador enters the ring for the third and final stage.

Stilt Racers and Spectators

In his cartoon sketch *The Stilts,* Goya portrays an event that made a strange yet exciting diversion during fiestas up to the 19th century. Men would race through the streets on long, rickety wooden stilts, followed by musicians playing flutes. The competitors in this picture (opposite) are wearing the *chaquetilla,* or short jacket, favored by the matador. Indeed, they may well be bullfighters, as this activity is almost as dangerous as facing an angry bull.

The two spectators near the front are wearing wide-brimmed sombreros and long, dark cloaks that cover their whole bodies. This was the standard dress of Madrid's well-to-do gentlemen of the time. In March of 1766, the government tried to pass a law banning the outfit, as it provided the perfect way to conceal a weapon and to disguise one's identity after committing a crime. However, major riots in response to the laws caused them to be dropped. This outfit was also featured in the *comedias de capa y espada,* or "comedies of cloak and sword," which were plays of murder and action written by Spanish dramatist Lope de Vega (1562–1635). The term *capa y espada* gave rise to our modern English phrase "cloak and dagger."

Stilt-walking still survives as a fiesta attraction. During the festival of Saint Mary Magdalene held every July in the province of Logroño, men perform an extravagant and daring dance—the *danza de los zancos*—on long stilts. The dancers spiral through the steep, cobbled streets dressed in wide, brightly colored skirts and striped vests covered in flowers—an impressive, if hazardous, spectacle.

Both these examples may have originated with Spanish shepherds, who would use stilts in order to keep a better watch over their flocks.

This drawing of *The Stilts* was completed by Goya as a preliminary sketch for a range of tapestries. The painting of the same scene shows the bright red of the stilt walkers' outfits against the browns and blacks of the spectators' clothes.

Music and Dance

Most regions of Spain have their own traditional folk dances and costumes, and these can be seen at local fiestas. Perhaps the most famous example is flamenco, an exciting form of song, dance, and music associated with the Andalucía region in southern Spain. It is thought that flamenco began as a folk song accompanied only by hand clapping, and that the guitar came later. The first performers of flamenco may have been Gypsy musicians, who began arriving in Spain from northern India (hence the Far Eastern tonality of the vocals) in the 15th century. However, the art was probably also influenced by local Andalucían folk music and by the music of the Moors who ruled Spain in the early Middle Ages.

The sultry and flamboyant costume of the female flamenco dancer has become famous all over the world. In its most practical form, the bodice is usually tightly fitted, while the skirt has four or five frilled layers and a train known as the *bata de cola.* This dress is usually made from plain or spotted cotton. Red is a popular color. A woman may also use a fan or castanets as part of the dance. A percussion instrument, the castanets (*castañeta* in Spanish) are two linked, shell-shaped pieces of hard wood held in the hand and sounded with rapid finger movements.

A fancier variation is the *sevillana* dress, which is extravagantly frilled on the skirt and arms and decorated with lace. Bright colors and floral designs complete the package. The *sevillana*-style dress is a familiar outfit at fiestas, especially in southern Spain. It is usually worn with

Men from the Galician province wear a white shirt and a red and black vest, with a red sash around the waist. Most noticeable is the long triangular hat with two pom-poms, one on top and one on the side.

Galician women tend to wear red skirts with bands of black velvet around the hem. A black or colored apron decorated with lace is worn over this. The white blouse has a high neckline and is covered by a shawl that repeats the use of red and black in the skirt.

hair combs, which were first used by matadors but later adopted by women. Another hair accessory is the flower. Different types are chosen, depending on the color of the dress and the blooms in fashion at the time.

The male flamenco costume is usually much less opulent. Tight black trousers extend above the waist. Then, somewhat like the matador, there is a short vest and jacket, which can be in a variety of colors. Both male and female dancers wear sturdy shoes, often with nails hammered into the soles to provide a percussion noise, like tap dancers.

Customs of the North

Around 2,600 years ago, Celtic tribes occupied the region of Galicia, in the far northwest of Spain. The traditions of this area owe much to this invasion. A variety of folk music styles can be heard here, but the key instrument is the *gaita,* a Spanish version of the bagpipes. This is an ancient Celtic wind instrument associated with Scotland. The *gaita* is accompanied by a drum and tambourine, which are part of the traditional Celtic music of Ireland.

Perhaps the most popular form of folk dance in the region is the *muñeira,* a Gaelic-style jig accompanied by jaunty, upbeat music. It has been suggested that the *muñeira* originated as a courting dance performed by young couples as they waited to grind their grain in the local mill (*muñeira* means "miller girl"). At the regular festivals and folk music events held throughout Galicia, the *muñeira* is often performed in traditional regional costume.

Portugal

Portugal takes up most of the western seaboard of the Iberian Peninsula and supports a population of around 10 million. Like Spain, many different peoples have colonized the country during its history. Celts, Romans, Visigoths, and Moors have each added to Portugal's heritage, still evident today.

As early as the Iron Age, hundreds of years before Christ, Celts came from northern Europe and settled in northern Portugal, which still retains some Celtic customs to this day. Later, the Romans colonized the whole country, bringing their advanced engineering, architecture, and legal systems. In the sixth century A.D., a deteriorating Roman Empire allowed the Visigoths to gain control of the whole peninsula, although this Germanic tribe had less effect on Portugal than it had on Spain. Finally, in A.D. 710, came the Moors from North Africa, bringing their religion of Islam, various elements of African culture, and, vitally, a highly evolved knowledge of shipbuilding and navigation. Christian armies began driving the Moors out of the peninsula in the 9th and 10th centuries, but there still remains a strong North African influence in the south of the country.

The wealthy Portuguese royalty could be lavishly dressed, as seen here, with the fur-lined jacket and heavy gold chain. The crown reflects the Portuguese preference for wide-brimmed hats.

The Dress of the *Festa*

Most regions of Portugal have their own traditional clothes, which are worn only during festivals—or *festas* as they are known there. The most recognizable is the costume of the Minho region, in the northwest of the country. There, women wear a long, richly colored skirt made from linen and wool. Underneath it are usually several underskirts or petticoats that give the skirt a fuller appearance.

Over the skirt is the traditional apron. Sometimes, this is plainly colored at the top and lavishly embroidered at the bottom, with different-colored squares woven into the material. In another style, the apron is almost completely covered in detailed floral embroidery. The colors of the apron reveal which particular village the wearer comes from. She might also embroider the names of loved ones onto the pockets on the front of the apron.

A young woman from Vianna in Portugal's Minho region wears a traditional outfit. It is completed with a pair of white stockings and is usually accompanied by an embroidered pouch worn over the shoulder.

The rest of the outfit includes a bodice and, under that, a linen or cotton blouse with long sleeves and frills at the neck and sometimes at the cuff. A kerchief, tied back from the forehead, is also essential, and a shawl might be added to the ensemble for warmth. A pair of mule-skin shoes, which are usually finely embroidered with flowers and branches, are the traditional footwear. This outfit has become so familiar that many people think of it as the national costume of Portugal.

Typically, the male *festa* dress of Minho is much less colorful. Black trousers, a short black jacket with decorative white buttons, and a simple white shirt make up the standard apparel. A red sash is usually added around the waist, which is reminiscent of some of the Spanish traditional costumes. Indeed, the contrast of bright, rich female dress with dark, staid male dress is similar to the Spanish flamenco.

The Shoes of Minho

The traditional slip-on shoes of the Minho region were usually made from mule skin, and the uppers are richly embroidered with flowers to match the floral designs that often adorned the aprons. The shoes have comparatively tall heels and, therefore, would only have been worn for special occasions, such as religious festivals. They are usually worn with a pair of white stockings.

Jewelry of Portugal

The gold and silver jewelry below were all made in Portugal, probably in the 19th century. The style is chunky and ornate—often the earrings and pendants are made of articulated sections, which move separately from each other. Precious metals were easily available in Portugal, both from domestic mines and from conquered lands overseas. Consequently, this type of jewelry was reasonably cheap and accessible not only to the nobility, but also to townspeople. Filigree was a common feature of traditional Portuguese jewelry.

Jewelry

If you were to attend the *festa* of Nossa Senhora da Agonia (Our Lady of Sorrows) in Viana do Castelo, Minho, you would notice that, along with the traditional dress, women also wear an abundance of gold jewelry. Today, this is just for show, but in previous centuries, the amount of gold a young girl wore revealed to potential husbands how much money she could provide as a dowry. Indeed, parents would often invest their life savings in these chunky necklaces, pendants, and earrings to ensure a good marriage for their daughters.

The three most popular designs for jewelry are the bow, the cross, and the heart. The bow was a favorite design of Portuguese noblewomen before being adopted by ordinary folk. The heart probably comes from the order of the Sacred Heart of Jesus, well established in Portugal for hundreds of years.

This pair from Portugal's Minho region includes a woman in *festa* attire with parasol and felt hat. The man wears the standard wide-brimmed hat, jacket, waistcoat, and breeches.

Here are various tradespeople in the traditional dress of Portugal's fishing villages. The women—who sell fish, mussels, and shrimp—often roll their long blouse sleeves up to their elbows, probably to protect the garments while they work.

Everyday Clothing

The traditional regional clothing of Portugal has died out now, replaced by modern styles, but until the 20th century, the clothing Portuguese people wore told a lot about where they came from and what they did for a living.

The Mountain Dwellers

The farmers of Portugal's mountainous north were known for their simple clothing. In contrast to the vibrant colors of Minho's *festa* dress, they tended to wear brown or black. For both men and women, the

Madeira

Madeira is a small island about 620 miles (1,000 km) southwest of Portugal. Traditional costumes are still worn by the island's flower sellers. Women wear a red woolen dress with yellow, black, and white stripes. Beneath the red bodice is a simple white linen blouse, and over the top of both is a cape, which drapes over the shoulders and across the body. The men wear a white, baggy shirt and matching baggy breeches. Both wear goatskin or leather boots and a small cap with a long, thin taper, or pigtail, coming out of the top.

wide-brimmed felt hat was essential, usually with the brim curved inward at the sides. Men also wore a vest, a short jacket, and long breeches—all made of coarse brown wool—and a shirt of cotton or hemp. Beneath the breeches, and covering the tops of the shoes, the farmer wore a pair of gaiters, or *alpargatas,* as they were known locally.

Women wore a full skirt reaching down to the calves, usually covered by a plain brown apron. A corset covered their wide-sleeved white shirts. Around their shoulders they wore a *fichu,* a decorative lace shoulder garment popular with both the poor and the rich. Finally, both men and women wore simple, sturdy, wooden-soled shoes.

For *festas,* women modestly decorated their standard work clothes. They wore gold necklaces and black felt hats with pom-poms, and carried parasols. They would also hold up their long brown skirts to show off the white underskirts. Some wore a *capa,* or long cloak.

The cassock, or *vestis talaris,* worn by this priest has a long history in Portugal. In A.D. 572, the Council of Braga in the Minho region was the first Synod in Europe to make this required wear for the clergy.

The most interesting work costume of the mountain regions belonged to shepherds. They wore the usual brown vest and wide-brimmed hat, but their long cloaks were woven from several layers of reed. This ingenious garment, called a *coroca,* was actually fully waterproof—a great advantage in the rainy north.

The shepherds of central Portugal favored a different costume, perhaps because that part of the country is not quite as rainy. Here, the outfit included thick sheepskin **chaps** over their trousers, a quilted cotton jacket with blue and white plaids, and hardy leather shoes. They also wore cloth-stocking caps with tassels at the end—a variation on the Phrygian bonnet. A brown blanket was additionally thrown over one shoulder.

Fishermen

Fishing has been an important part of Portuguese life since the Romans occupied Iberia. Sardines are the main catch. They can be found all around the coast, and canned sardines remain one of modern Portugal's largest exports. Tuna is also fished, but it is mostly found in the seas nearest to the Algarve on the southern coast.

The traditional dress of the Portuguese fisherman is similar to the outfits their Italian equivalents wear: a baggy white shirt with open collar, loose white

The Civil War

The Portuguese Civil War (1832–1834) pitted liberal intellectuals against the oppressive regime of Prince Miguel. Many peasants of the Minho region joined the rebels, adapting their work clothes for conflict. Women wore the standard mountain peasant outfit of brown skirt, brown bodice, and white shirt with sleeves rolled up to the elbow. Instead of a low, wide-brimmed hat, they wore a high felt hat over a white handkerchief. For weapons, the peasants would carry a revolver and a spear or hatchet.

trousers, and a small cap. Until the modern era, neither men nor women of fishing communities wore shoes. Even today, bare feet are normal in many of the coastal villages.

For women, a full skirt of coarse brown cloth was standard wear, usually accompanied by a white cotton blouse. A *fichu* was commonly worn around the shoulders. This decorative garment, introduced in the late 18th century, looks like a short scarf and was usually made of lace. It was knotted loosely around the neck, with the points crossing at the chest.

A felt hat with an upturned brim was also a common sight. However, if anything needed to be carried, the hat would be replaced with a large basket, held in place on the top of the head with a padded kerchief. Women developed excellent poise and bearing due to the balance and strength this required. Even today, carrying goods on the head is the preferred method in villages found along Portugal's coast. Fishermen's wives from the town of Esposende made an interesting addition to the usual costume, attaching small mirrors to the front

The Stick Dancers

One of the strangest traditional costumes in Portugal is the outfit of the *pauliteiros* dancers of Miranda do Douro. Like the morris dancers of England, the men dance in groups with short sticks, which they bang together in time with the music. Instead of trousers, they wear frilly, white, three-tiered skirts and tie colorful scarves around their waists. Over their white shirts, each dancer wears a shawl decorated with flowers. The outfit is completed with a black hat, again decorated with flowers. Some believe the dance and costume originated with ancient Greek settlers.

of their black felt hats. As the women waited for their husbands to return from sea, the mirrors would flash in the sun, helping to guide the boats safely to shore.

Ecclesiastical Dress

Portugal, like Spain, is a primarily Christian country and religion is a vital part of family life. This devotion was tested in 1911 when the first republican government attempted to suppress the church, making religious education illegal. This policy invoked the wrath of the people and eventually led to the government's failure and the reversal of the antireligious policies. Today, 95 percent of the population is Catholic.

Until the 20th century, the state funded only the upper ranks of the church hierarchy, so the ordinary clergy relied on the *congrua*, a kind of **tithe** donated

The clergyman, second from right, is wearing a traditional cassock under his cloak. The three-cornered hat and the white robe under the black cloat on the man in the center indicates that this clergyman is a Dominican.

by parishioners. Their traditional dress is modest. It features a long **cassock** of brown cloth, tied at the waist with a wide belt that is knotted at the side. Over this is a long cloak. Completing the outfit are buckled shoes and a barrette hat with a pom-pom on the side.

Religious orders were well represented in Portugal until 1834, when a new government regime abolished the monasteries. Each order wore variations on the typical monk's robes. The brothers of the Saint Anthony and Carmelite orders wore the most simple outfits, consisting of brown robes, hooded cloaks, and rope belts. Dominican friars wore a black cloak fastened at the neck over a long white robe. They also carried rosary beads suspended from their belts. Finally, Benedictine monks favored a voluminous black outer garment that completely covered their black robes. All wore the typical Portuguese wide-brimmed hat, aside from the Dominicans, who chose a three-cornered hat.

Glossary

Note: Specialized words relating to clothing are explained within the text, but those that appear more than once are listed below for easy reference.

Alluvial plain agricultural area rich in alluvium, a type of soil rich in mineral deposits left behind by floodwaters

Alpargatas gaiters worn beneath the breeches and covering the tops of shoes

Archipelago a group of islands

Articulated having a hinged connection

Batiste fine cotton or linen

Breeches short pants covering the hips and thighs and fitting snugly at the lower edges at or just below the knee

Cartoon originally, this meant a series of paintings on a similar theme, typically commissioned to decorate a single room

Cassock a long black or red robe worn by the clergy

Caste a division of society based on differences of wealth, inherited rank or privilege, profession, or occupation

Chaps leather leggings joined by a belt or lacing, often having flared outer flaps, and worn over the trousers

Codpiece a flap or bag concealing an opening in the front of men's breeches

Corset a close-fitting supporting undergarment that is often hooked and laced and that extends from above or beneath the bust or from the waist to below the hips

Doublet a short, close-fitting, often padded jacket

Dowry a gift of money, property, or jewelry traditionally provided by the family of the bride for the bridegroom

Ecclesiastical relating to the church

Espadrilles lightweight canvas shoes, usually with a coarse fabric sole

Fichu a woman's light triangular scarf that is draped over the shoulders and fastened in front or worn to fill in a low neckline

Frock coat a man's knee-length, usually double-breasted, coat

Gaiters a cloth or leather leg covering reaching from the instep to above the ankle or to mid-calf or knee

Gorget a decorative garment covering the neck, usually made from silk, cotton, or fur

Guard arms pieces of metal usually fashioned into an S shape and attached to the handle of a sword to protect the hand of the swordsman

Heretic a person who defies established religious dogma

Morris dancers English dancers, whose dances have their roots in pagan rituals of fertility

Mudéjar of, or relating to, the Moorish population of Spain; usually refers to arabesque architecture or art from that period

Nomadic characteristic of a people who have no permanent location

Paella a meal of rice and seafood seasoned with saffron, which turns it yellow, and cooked in a pan; often referred to as Spain's national dish

Pannier a type of underskirt shaped with metal hoops

Phrygian bonnet a pointed hat that originated in ancient Asia Minor; the point is sometimes folded over toward the front

Reconquista Spanish for "reconquest"; refers to the Christian fight to win back Spain from the Moors during the Middle Ages

Tithe a tenth part of something paid as a voluntary contribution or as a tax, especially for the support of a religious establishment

Timeline

700 B.C.	Celtic tribes settle in the north of Spain and Portugal.
A.D. 419	Visigoths invade the Iberian Peninsula and establish a kingdom.
711	Moorish forces invade Spain and defeat the Visigoth king; the Moors bring silk and arabesque designs to the country.

800s The tomb of the apostle Saint James the Great is discovered in Santiago de Compostela; pilgrims come to Spain from all over Europe, bringing new fashions to the country.

1100s Portugal becomes an independent nation.

1200s Early Christian kings of Spain combine Visigoth and Moorish elements in their dress.

1400s Portuguese explorers sail around Africa and toward India, bringing back new textiles and fashions from the East; Romany Gypsies begin to settle in southern Spain.

1419 The Portuguese claim the Madeira Islands.

1492 Christian forces overthrow the last Moorish bastion in Granada; Christopher Columbus discovers the New World.

1500s Spain's golden age of colonial expansion; the arts flourish; Spanish fashion dominates Europe; Spain claims the Philippines as part of its empire and brings back the *manton de Manila* from this region.

1580 Philip II of Spain becomes king of Portugal; the two countries are united for 60 years.

1588 The British fleet destroys the Spanish Armada.

1700s Bullfighting develops as a *fiesta* attraction throughout Spain.

1788 Francisco Goya begins to paint Madrid society; his works show the fashions of the era.

1800s Flamenco becomes popular throughout Spain.

1814 The French are expelled from Spain.

1832–1834 Portuguese Civil War leads to the dissolution of the monasteries.

1843–1868 Queen Isabella II popularizes the lace mantilla.

1898 The Spanish–American War sees Spain lose the last of its New World colonies.

1910 Portugal becomes a republic.

1936–1939   The Spanish Civil War; General Francisco Franco is installed as dictator.

1975   Franco dies; King Juan Carlos I brings in a constitutional monarchy.

Online Sources

Bullfighting
http://mundo-taurino.org/
Information on bullfighting in Spain and elsewhere.

Catholic history
http://www.newadvent.org/cathen
A Catholic encyclopedia with a lot of information on the history of Spain and Portugal.

Flamenco
http://www.flamenco.org
A guide to the music and costume of flamenco.

European culture
http://www.eun.org/eun.org2/eun/index_myeurope.cfm
A vast educational site on European culture with resources relating to traditional dress.

Islam
http://www.al-islam.org/
A useful introduction to Islam, the religion of the Moors.

Spain and Portugal
http://www.spanish-living.com/
http://www.red2000.com/spain/index.html
http://www.portugal.org/indexhtml/index2.html
A selection of good sites with information on the customs and traditions of these two countries.

Costume and fashion
http://www.costumes.org/pages/costhistpage.htm
http://moas.atlantia.sca.org/topics/clot.htm
Two huge lists of links to various sites dealing with costume history from around the world.

Further Reading

Boucher, François. *20,000 Years of Fashion: The History of Fashion and Personal Adornment.* New York: Abrams, 1987.

Bown, Deni. *Eyewitness Travel Guide to Spain.* New York: Dorling Kindersley, 2001.

Harrold, Robert, and Phyllida Legg. *Folk Costumes of the World.* Herndon, Va.: Cassell Academic, 1999.

Hemingway, Ernest. *Death in the Afternoon.* New York: Touchstone Books, 1999.

Nicolle, David, and Angus McBride. *The Moors: The Islamic West 7th–15th Centuries A.D. (Men-at-Arms 348).* Oxford: Osprey, 2001.

About the Author

Keith Stuart graduated from the University of Warwick in 1994. The history of European theatrical and traditional costume formed a significant element of his BA (Hons) degree in English Literature and Theater. He is a prolific writer and journalist, contributing to several lifestyle and culture magazines, as well as the national newspaper, *The Guardian.* He is a regular writer for respected art magazine *Frieze.* Stuart has also travelled extensively throughout Europe, writing on German, Italian, and Russian culture.

Index